U.S. NATIO

① ACADIA
② AMERICAN SAMOA
③ ARCHES
④ BADLANDS
⑤ BIG BEND
⑥ BISCAYNE
⑦ BLACK CANYON OF THE GUNNISON
⑧ BRYCE CANYON
⑨ CANYONLANDS
⑩ CAPITOL REEF
⑪ CARLSBAD CAVERNS
⑫ CHANNEL ISLANDS
⑬ CONGAREE
⑭ CRATER LAKE
⑮ CUYAHOGA VALLEY
⑯ DEATH VALLEY
⑰ DENALI
⑱ DRY TORTUGAS
⑲ EVERGLADES
⑳ GATES OF THE ARCTIC
㉑ GATEWAY ARCH
㉒ GLACIER
㉓ GLACIER BAY
㉔ GRAND CANYON
㉕ GRAND TETON
㉖ GREAT BASIN
㉗ GREAT SAND DUNES
㉘ GREAT SMOKY MOUNTAINS
㉙ GUADALUPE MOUNTAINS
㉚ HALEAKALA
㉛ HAWAI'I VOLCANOES
㉜ HOT SPRINGS
㉝ INDIANA DUNES
㉞ ISLE ROYALE
㉟ JOSHUA TREE
㊱ KATMAI
㊲ KENAI FJORDS
㊳ KINGS CANYON
㊴ KOBUK VALLEY
㊵ LAKE CLARK
㊶ LASSEN VOLCANIC
㊷ MAMMOTH CAVE
㊸ MESA VERDE
㊹ MOUNT RAINIER
㊺ NORTH CASCADES
㊻ OLYMPIC
㊼ PETRIFIED FOREST
㊽ PINNACLES
㊾ REDWOOD
㊿ ROCKY MOUNTAIN
(51) SAGUARO
(52) SEQUOIA
(53) SHENANDOAH
(54) THEODORE ROOSEVELT
(55) VIRGIN ISLANDS
(56) VOYAGEURS
(57) WIND CAVE
(58) WRANGELL-ST. ELIAS
(59) YELLOWSTONE
(60) YOSEMITE
(61) ZION

U.S. NATIONAL PARKS TRACKING LOG

	U.S. NATIONAL PARK	LOCATION	ESTABLISHED	DATE(S) VISITED
○	ACADIA	MAINE	1919	
○	AMERICAN SAMOA	AMERICAN SAMOA	1988	
○	ARCHES	UTAH	1971	
○	BADLANDS	SOUTH DAKOTA	1978	
○	BIG BEND	TEXAS	1944	
○	BISCAYNE	FLORIDA	1980	
○	BLACK CANYON OF THE GUNNISON	COLORADO	1999	
○	BRYCE CANYON	UTAH	1928	
○	CANYONLANDS	UTAH	1964	
○	CAPITOL REEF	UTAH	1971	
○	CARLSBAD CAVERNS	NEW MEXICO	1930	
○	CHANNEL ISLANDS	CALIFORNIA	1980	
○	CONGAREE	SOUTH CAROLINA	2003	
○	CRATER LAKE	OREGON	1902	
○	CUYAHOGA VALLEY	OHIO	2000	
○	DEATH VALLEY	CALIFORNIA/NEVADA	1994	
○	DENALI	ALASKA	1917	
○	DRY TORTUGAS	FLORIDA	1992	
○	EVERGLADES	FLORIDA	1934	
○	GATES OF THE ARCTIC	ALASKA	1980	
○	GATEWAY ARCH	MISSOURI	2018	
○	GLACIER	MONTANA	1910	
○	GLACIER BAY	ALASKA	1980	
○	GRAND CANYON	ARIZONA	1919	
○	GRAND TETON	WYOMING	1929	
○	GREAT BASIN	NEVADA	1986	
○	GREAT SAND DUNES	COLORADO	2004	
○	GREAT SMOKY MOUNTAINS	TENNESSEE/NORTH CAROLINA	1934	
○	GUADALUPE MOUNTAINS	TEXAS	1966	
○	HALEAKALĀ	HAWAII	1916	

	U.S. NATIONAL PARK	LOCATION	ESTABLISHED	DATE(S) VISITED
○	**HAWAI'I VOLCANOES**	HAWAII	1916	
○	**HOT SPRINGS**	ARKANSAS	1921	
○	**INDIANA DUNES**	INDIANA	2019	
○	**ISLE ROYALE**	MICHIGAN	1940	
○	**JOSHUA TREE**	CALIFORNIA	1994	
○	**KATMAI**	ALASKA	1980	
○	**KENAI FJORDS**	ALASKA	1980	
○	**KINGS CANYON**	CALIFORNIA	1940	
○	**KOBUK VALLEY**	ALASKA	1980	
○	**LAKE CLARK**	ALASKA	1980	
○	**LASSEN VOLCANIC**	CALIFORNIA	1916	
○	**MAMMOTH CAVE**	KENTUCKY	1941	
○	**MESA VERDE**	COLORADO	1906	
○	**MOUNT RAINIER**	WASHINGTON	1899	
○	**NORTH CASCADES**	WASHINGTON	1968	
○	**OLYMPIC**	WASHINGTON	1938	
○	**PETRIFIED FOREST**	ARIZONA	1962	
○	**PINNACLES**	CALIFORNIA	2013	
○	**REDWOOD**	CALIFORNIA	1968	
○	**ROCKY MOUNTAIN**	COLORADO	1915	
○	**SAGUARO**	ARIZONA	1994	
○	**SEQUOIA**	CALIFORNIA	1890	
○	**SHENANDOAH**	VIRGINIA	1935	
○	**THEODORE ROOSEVELT**	NORTH DAKOTA	1978	
○	**VIRGIN ISLANDS**	U.S. VIRGIN ISLANDS	1956	
○	**VOYAGEURS**	MINNESOTA	1971	
○	**WIND CAVE**	SOUTH DAKOTA	1903	
○	**WRANGELL-ST. ELIAS**	ALASKA	1980	
○	**YELLOWSTONE**	WYOMING/MONTANA/IDAHO	1872	
○	**YOSEMITE**	CALIFORNIA	1890	
○	**ZION**	UTAH	1919	

ACADIA
NATIONAL PARK

CITY/STATE ENTERED:

DATES VISITED:

WEATHER:

WHO WAS WITH ME:

WHERE WE STAYED:

WHAT WE DID:

MY FAVORITE MEMORY

SIGHTS:

WILDLIFE:

HIKES/STORIES/ADVENTURES:

I WOULD RATE THIS NATIONAL PARK:

☆ ☆ ☆ ☆ ☆ ☆ ☆ ☆ ☆ ☆

NOTES FOR NEXT TIME:

VISIT AGAIN?

YES   NO

PASSPORT STAMPS

AMERICAN SAMOA
NATIONAL PARK

CITY/STATE ENTERED:

DATES VISITED:

WEATHER:

WHO WAS WITH ME:

WHERE WE STAYED:

WHAT WE DID:

MY FAVORITE MEMORY

SIGHTS:

WILDLIFE:

HIKES/STORIES/ADVENTURES:

I WOULD RATE THIS NATIONAL PARK:

☆ ☆ ☆ ☆ ☆ ☆ ☆ ☆ ☆ ☆

NOTES FOR NEXT TIME:

VISIT
AGAIN?

YES   NO

PASSPORT STAMPS

ARCHES
NATIONAL PARK

CITY/STATE ENTERED:

DATES VISITED:

WEATHER:

WHO WAS WITH ME:

WHERE WE STAYED:

WHAT WE DID:

MY FAVORITE MEMORY

SIGHTS:

WILDLIFE:

HIKES/STORIES/ADVENTURES:

I WOULD RATE THIS NATIONAL PARK:

☆ ☆ ☆ ☆ ☆ ☆ ☆ ☆ ☆ ☆

NOTES FOR NEXT TIME:

VISIT
AGAIN?

YES   NO

PASSPORT STAMPS

BADLANDS
NATIONAL PARK

CITY/STATE ENTERED:

DATES VISITED:

WEATHER:

WHO WAS WITH ME:

WHERE WE STAYED:

WHAT WE DID:

MY FAVORITE MEMORY

SIGHTS:

WILDLIFE:

HIKES/STORIES/ADVENTURES:

I WOULD RATE THIS NATIONAL PARK:

☆ ☆ ☆ ☆ ☆ ☆ ☆ ☆ ☆ ☆

NOTES FOR NEXT TIME:

VISIT AGAIN?

YES   NO

PASSPORT STAMPS

BIG BEND
NATIONAL PARK

CITY/STATE ENTERED:

DATES VISITED:

WEATHER:

WHO WAS WITH ME:

WHERE WE STAYED:

WHAT WE DID:

MY FAVORITE MEMORY

SIGHTS:

WILDLIFE:

HIKES/STORIES/ADVENTURES:

I WOULD RATE THIS NATIONAL PARK:

☆ ☆ ☆ ☆ ☆ ☆ ☆ ☆ ☆ ☆

NOTES FOR NEXT TIME:

VISIT AGAIN?

YES   NO

PASSPORT STAMPS

BISCAYNE
NATIONAL PARK

CITY/STATE ENTERED:

DATES VISITED:

WEATHER:

WHO WAS WITH ME:

WHERE WE STAYED:

WHAT WE DID:

MY FAVORITE MEMORY

SIGHTS:

WILDLIFE:

HIKES/STORIES/ADVENTURES:

I WOULD RATE THIS NATIONAL PARK:

☆ ☆ ☆ ☆ ☆ ☆ ☆ ☆ ☆ ☆

NOTES FOR NEXT TIME:

VISIT AGAIN?

YES   NO

PASSPORT STAMPS

BLACK CANYON OF THE GUNNISON

CITY/STATE ENTERED:

DATES VISITED:

WEATHER:

WHO WAS WITH ME:

WHERE WE STAYED:

WHAT WE DID:

MY FAVORITE MEMORY

SIGHTS:

WILDLIFE:

HIKES/STORIES/ADVENTURES:

I WOULD RATE THIS NATIONAL PARK:

☆ ☆ ☆ ☆ ☆ ☆ ☆ ☆ ☆ ☆

NOTES FOR NEXT TIME:

VISIT AGAIN?

YES   NO

PASSPORT STAMPS

BRYCE CANYON
NATIONAL PARK

● ● ● ● ● ● ● ● ● ● ● ● ● ● ● ● ● ● ●

CITY/STATE ENTERED:

DATES VISITED:

WEATHER:

WHO WAS WITH ME:

WHERE WE STAYED:

WHAT WE DID:

MY FAVORITE MEMORY

SIGHTS:

WILDLIFE:

HIKES/STORIES/ADVENTURES:

I WOULD RATE THIS NATIONAL PARK:

☆ ☆ ☆ ☆ ☆ ☆ ☆ ☆ ☆ ☆

NOTES FOR NEXT TIME:

VISIT
AGAIN?

YES   NO

PASSPORT STAMPS

CANYONLANDS
NATIONAL PARK

CITY/STATE ENTERED:

DATES VISITED:

WEATHER:

WHO WAS WITH ME:

WHERE WE STAYED:

WHAT WE DID:

MY FAVORITE MEMORY

SIGHTS:

WILDLIFE:

HIKES/STORIES/ADVENTURES:

I WOULD RATE THIS NATIONAL PARK:

☆ ☆ ☆ ☆ ☆ ☆ ☆ ☆ ☆ ☆

NOTES FOR NEXT TIME:

VISIT AGAIN?

YES   NO

PASSPORT STAMPS

CAPITOL REEF
NATIONAL PARK

CITY/STATE ENTERED:

DATES VISITED:

WEATHER:

WHO WAS WITH ME:

WHERE WE STAYED:

WHAT WE DID:

MY FAVORITE MEMORY

SIGHTS:

WILDLIFE:

HIKES/STORIES/ADVENTURES:

I WOULD RATE THIS NATIONAL PARK:

☆ ☆ ☆ ☆ ☆ ☆ ☆ ☆ ☆ ☆

NOTES FOR NEXT TIME:

VISIT AGAIN?

YES   NO

PASSPORT STAMPS

CARLSBAD CAVERNS
NATIONAL PARK

CITY/STATE ENTERED:

DATES VISITED:

WEATHER:

WHO WAS WITH ME:

WHERE WE STAYED:

WHAT WE DID:

MY FAVORITE MEMORY

SIGHTS:

WILDLIFE:

HIKES/STORIES/ADVENTURES:

I WOULD RATE THIS NATIONAL PARK:

☆ ☆ ☆ ☆ ☆ ☆ ☆ ☆ ☆ ☆

NOTES FOR NEXT TIME:

VISIT AGAIN?

YES   NO

PASSPORT STAMPS

CHANNEL ISLANDS
NATIONAL PARK

CITY/STATE ENTERED:

DATES VISITED:

WEATHER:

WHO WAS WITH ME:

WHERE WE STAYED:

WHAT WE DID:

MY FAVORITE MEMORY

SIGHTS:

WILDLIFE:

HIKES/STORIES/ADVENTURES:

I WOULD RATE THIS NATIONAL PARK:

☆ ☆ ☆ ☆ ☆ ☆ ☆ ☆ ☆ ☆

NOTES FOR NEXT TIME:

VISIT AGAIN?

YES   NO

PASSPORT STAMPS

CONGAREE
NATIONAL PARK

CITY/STATE ENTERED:

DATES VISITED:

WEATHER:

WHO WAS WITH ME:

WHERE WE STAYED:

WHAT WE DID:

MY FAVORITE MEMORY

SIGHTS:

WILDLIFE:

HIKES/STORIES/ADVENTURES:

I WOULD RATE THIS NATIONAL PARK:

☆ ☆ ☆ ☆ ☆ ☆ ☆ ☆ ☆ ☆

NOTES FOR NEXT TIME:

VISIT AGAIN?

YES   NO

PASSPORT STAMPS

CRATER LAKE
NATIONAL PARK

CITY/STATE ENTERED:

DATES VISITED:

WEATHER:

WHO WAS WITH ME:

WHERE WE STAYED:

WHAT WE DID:

MY FAVORITE MEMORY

SIGHTS:

WILDLIFE:

HIKES/STORIES/ADVENTURES:

I WOULD RATE THIS NATIONAL PARK:

☆ ☆ ☆ ☆ ☆ ☆ ☆ ☆ ☆ ☆

NOTES FOR NEXT TIME:

VISIT AGAIN?

YES   NO

PASSPORT STAMPS

CUYAHOGA VALLEY
NATICNAL PARK

CITY/STATE ENTERED:

DATES VISITED:

WEATHER:

WHO WAS WITH ME:

WHERE WE STAYED:

WHAT WE DID:

MY FAVORITE MEMORY

SIGHTS:

WILDLIFE:

HIKES/STORIES/ADVENTURES:

I WOULD RATE THIS NATIONAL PARK:

☆ ☆ ☆ ☆ ☆ ☆ ☆ ☆ ☆ ☆

NOTES FOR NEXT TIME:

VISIT AGAIN?

YES   NO

PASSPORT STAMPS

DEATH VALLEY
NATIONAL PARK

CITY/STATE ENTERED:

DATES VISITED:

WEATHER:

WHO WAS WITH ME:

WHERE WE STAYED:

WHAT WE DID:

MY FAVORITE MEMORY

SIGHTS:

WILDLIFE:

HIKES/STORIES/ADVENTURES:

I WOULD RATE THIS NATIONAL PARK:

☆ ☆ ☆ ☆ ☆ ☆ ☆ ☆ ☆ ☆

NOTES FOR NEXT TIME:

VISIT
AGAIN?

YES   NO

PASSPORT STAMPS

DENALI
NATIONAL PARK

CITY/STATE ENTERED:

DATES VISITED:

WEATHER:

WHO WAS WITH ME:

WHERE WE STAYED:

WHAT WE DID:

MY FAVORITE MEMORY

SIGHTS:

WILDLIFE:

HIKES/STORIES/ADVENTURES:

I WOULD RATE THIS NATIONAL PARK:

☆ ☆ ☆ ☆ ☆ ☆ ☆ ☆ ☆ ☆

NOTES FOR NEXT TIME:

VISIT AGAIN?

YES   NO

PASSPORT STAMPS

DRY TORTUGAS
NATIONAL PARK

CITY/STATE ENTERED:

DATES VISITED:

WEATHER:

WHO WAS WITH ME:

WHERE WE STAYED:

WHAT WE DID:

MY FAVORITE MEMORY

SIGHTS:

WILDLIFE:

HIKES/STORIES/ADVENTURES:

I WOULD RATE THIS NATIONAL PARK:

☆ ☆ ☆ ☆ ☆ ☆ ☆ ☆ ☆ ☆

NOTES FOR NEXT TIME:

VISIT
AGAIN?

YES   NO

PASSPORT STAMPS

EVERGLADES
NATIONAL PARK

CITY/STATE ENTERED:

DATES VISITED:

WEATHER:

WHO WAS WITH ME:

WHERE WE STAYED:

WHAT WE DID:

MY FAVORITE MEMORY

SIGHTS:

WILDLIFE:

HIKES/STORIES/ADVENTURES:

I WOULD RATE THIS NATIONAL PARK:

☆ ☆ ☆ ☆ ☆ ☆ ☆ ☆ ☆ ☆

NOTES FOR NEXT TIME:

VISIT AGAIN?

YES   NO

PASSPORT STAMPS

GATES OF THE ARCTIC
NATIONAL PARK

CITY/STATE ENTERED:

DATES VISITED:

WEATHER:

WHO WAS WITH ME:

WHERE WE STAYED:

WHAT WE DID:

MY FAVORITE MEMORY

SIGHTS:

WILDLIFE:

HIKES/STORIES/ADVENTURES:

I WOULD RATE THIS NATIONAL PARK:

☆ ☆ ☆ ☆ ☆ ☆ ☆ ☆ ☆ ☆

NOTES FOR NEXT TIME:

VISIT AGAIN?

YES   NO

PASSPORT STAMPS

GATEWAY ARCH
NATIONAL PARK

CITY/STATE ENTERED:

DATES VISITED:

WEATHER:

WHO WAS WITH ME:

WHERE WE STAYED:

WHAT WE DID:

MY FAVORITE MEMORY

SIGHTS:

WILDLIFE:

HIKES/STORIES/ADVENTURES:

I WOULD RATE THIS NATIONAL PARK:

☆ ☆ ☆ ☆ ☆ ☆ ☆ ☆ ☆ ☆

NOTES FOR NEXT TIME:

VISIT AGAIN?

YES   NO

PASSPORT STAMPS

GLACIER
NATIONAL PARK

CITY/STATE ENTERED:

DATES VISITED:

WEATHER:

WHO WAS WITH ME:

WHERE WE STAYED:

WHAT WE DID:

MY FAVORITE MEMORY

SIGHTS:

WILDLIFE:

HIKES/STORIES/ADVENTURES:

I WOULD RATE THIS NATIONAL PARK:

☆ ☆ ☆ ☆ ☆ ☆ ☆ ☆ ☆ ☆

NOTES FOR NEXT TIME:

VISIT AGAIN?

YES   NO

PASSPORT STAMPS

GLACIER BAY
NATIONAL PARK

CITY/STATE ENTERED:

DATES VISITED:

WEATHER:

WHO WAS WITH ME:

WHERE WE STAYED:

WHAT WE DID:

MY FAVORITE MEMORY

SIGHTS:

WILDLIFE:

HIKES/STORIES/ADVENTURES:

I WOULD RATE THIS NATIONAL PARK:

☆ ☆ ☆ ☆ ☆ ☆ ☆ ☆ ☆ ☆

NOTES FOR NEXT TIME:

VISIT AGAIN?

YES   NO

PASSPORT STAMPS

GRAND CANYON
NATIONAL PARK

CITY/STATE ENTERED:

DATES VISITED:

WEATHER:

WHO WAS WITH ME:

WHERE WE STAYED:

WHAT WE DID:

MY FAVORITE MEMORY

SIGHTS:

WILDLIFE:

HIKES/STORIES/ADVENTURES:

I WOULD RATE THIS NATIONAL PARK:

☆ ☆ ☆ ☆ ☆ ☆ ☆ ☆ ☆ ☆

NOTES FOR NEXT TIME:

VISIT AGAIN?

YES   NO

PASSPORT STAMPS

GRAND TETON
NATIONAL PARK

CITY/STATE ENTERED:

DATES VISITED:

WEATHER:

WHO WAS WITH ME:

WHERE WE STAYED:

WHAT WE DID:

MY FAVORITE MEMORY

SIGHTS:

WILDLIFE:

HIKES/STORIES/ADVENTURES:

I WOULD RATE THIS NATIONAL PARK:

☆ ☆ ☆ ☆ ☆ ☆ ☆ ☆ ☆ ☆

NOTES FOR NEXT TIME:

VISIT AGAIN?

YES   NO

PASSPORT STAMPS

GREAT BASIN
NATIONAL PARK

CITY/STATE ENTERED:

DATES VISITED:

WEATHER:

WHO WAS WITH ME:

WHERE WE STAYED:

WHAT WE DID:

MY FAVORITE MEMORY

SIGHTS:

WILDLIFE:

HIKES/STORIES/ADVENTURES:

I WOULD RATE THIS NATIONAL PARK:

☆ ☆ ☆ ☆ ☆ ☆ ☆ ☆ ☆ ☆

NOTES FOR NEXT TIME:

VISIT AGAIN?

YES   NO

PASSPORT STAMPS

GREAT SAND DUNES
NATIONAL PARK

CITY/STATE ENTERED:

DATES VISITED:

WEATHER:

WHO WAS WITH ME:

WHERE WE STAYED:

WHAT WE DID:

MY FAVORITE MEMORY

SIGHTS:

WILDLIFE:

HIKES/STORIES/ADVENTURES:

I WOULD RATE THIS NATIONAL PARK:

☆ ☆ ☆ ☆ ☆ ☆ ☆ ☆ ☆ ☆

NOTES FOR NEXT TIME:

VISIT AGAIN?

YES   NO

PASSPORT STAMPS

GREAT SMOKY MOUNTAINS

CITY/STATE ENTERED:

DATES VISITED:

WEATHER:

WHO WAS WITH ME:

WHERE WE STAYED:

WHAT WE DID:

MY FAVORITE MEMORY

SIGHTS:

WILDLIFE:

HIKES/STORIES/ADVENTURES:

I WOULD RATE THIS NATIONAL PARK:

☆ ☆ ☆ ☆ ☆ ☆ ☆ ☆ ☆ ☆

NOTES FOR NEXT TIME:

VISIT AGAIN?

YES   NO

PASSPORT STAMPS

GUADALUPE MOUNTAINS

CITY/STATE ENTERED:

DATES VISITED:

WEATHER:

WHO WAS WITH ME:

WHERE WE STAYED:

WHAT WE DID:

MY FAVORITE MEMORY

SIGHTS:

WILDLIFE:

HIKES/STORIES/ADVENTURES:

I WOULD RATE THIS NATIONAL PARK:

☆ ☆ ☆ ☆ ☆ ☆ ☆ ☆ ☆ ☆

NOTES FOR NEXT TIME:

VISIT AGAIN?

YES   NO

PASSPORT STAMPS

HALEAKALĀ
NATIONAL PARK

CITY/STATE ENTERED:

DATES VISITED:

WEATHER:

WHO WAS WITH ME:

WHERE WE STAYED:

WHAT WE DID:

MY FAVORITE MEMORY

SIGHTS:

WILDLIFE:

HIKES/STORIES/ADVENTURES:

I WOULD RATE THIS NATIONAL PARK:

☆ ☆ ☆ ☆ ☆ ☆ ☆ ☆ ☆ ☆

NOTES FOR NEXT TIME:

VISIT AGAIN?

YES   NO

PASSPORT STAMPS

HAWAI'I VOLCANOES
NATIONAL PARK

CITY/STATE ENTERED:

DATES VISITED:

WEATHER:

WHO WAS WITH ME:

WHERE WE STAYED:

WHAT WE DID:

MY FAVORITE MEMORY

SIGHTS:

WILDLIFE:

HIKES/STORIES/ADVENTURES:

I WOULD RATE THIS NATIONAL PARK:

☆ ☆ ☆ ☆ ☆ ☆ ☆ ☆ ☆ ☆

NOTES FOR NEXT TIME:

VISIT AGAIN?

YES   NO

PASSPORT STAMPS

HOT SPRINGS
NATIONAL PARK

CITY/STATE ENTERED:

DATES VISITED:

WEATHER:

WHO WAS WITH ME:

WHERE WE STAYED:

WHAT WE DID:

MY FAVORITE MEMORY

SIGHTS:

WILDLIFE:

HIKES/STORIES/ADVENTURES:

I WOULD RATE THIS NATIONAL PARK:

☆ ☆ ☆ ☆ ☆ ☆ ☆ ☆ ☆ ☆

NOTES FOR NEXT TIME:

VISIT
AGAIN?

YES   NO

PASSPORT STAMPS

INDIANA DUNES
NATIONAL PARK

CITY/STATE ENTERED:

DATES VISITED:

WEATHER:

WHO WAS WITH ME:

WHERE WE STAYED:

WHAT WE DID:

MY FAVORITE MEMORY

SIGHTS:

WILDLIFE:

HIKES/STORIES/ADVENTURES:

I WOULD RATE THIS NATIONAL PARK:

☆ ☆ ☆ ☆ ☆ ☆ ☆ ☆ ☆ ☆

NOTES FOR NEXT TIME:

VISIT AGAIN?

YES   NO

PASSPORT STAMPS

ISLE ROYALE
NATIONAL PARK

DATES VISITED:

CITY/STATE ENTERED:

WEATHER:

WHO WAS WITH ME:

WHERE WE STAYED:

WHAT WE DID:

MY FAVORITE MEMORY

SIGHTS:

WILDLIFE:

HIKES/STORIES/ADVENTURES:

I WOULD RATE THIS NATIONAL PARK:

☆ ☆ ☆ ☆ ☆ ☆ ☆ ☆ ☆ ☆

NOTES FOR NEXT TIME:

VISIT AGAIN?

YES   NO

PASSPORT STAMPS

JOSHUA TREE
NATIONAL PARK

DATES VISITED:

CITY/STATE ENTERED:

WEATHER:

WHO WAS WITH ME:

WHERE WE STAYED:

WHAT WE DID:

MY FAVORITE MEMORY

SIGHTS:

WILDLIFE:

HIKES/STORIES/ADVENTURES:

I WOULD RATE THIS NATIONAL PARK:

☆ ☆ ☆ ☆ ☆ ☆ ☆ ☆ ☆ ☆

NOTES FOR NEXT TIME:

VISIT AGAIN?

YES   NO

PASSPORT STAMPS

KATMAI
NATIONAL PARK

CITY/STATE ENTERED:

DATES VISITED:

WEATHER:

WHO WAS WITH ME:

WHERE WE STAYED:

WHAT WE DID:

MY FAVORITE MEMORY

SIGHTS:

WILDLIFE:

HIKES/STORIES/ADVENTURES:

I WOULD RATE THIS NATIONAL PARK:

☆ ☆ ☆ ☆ ☆ ☆ ☆ ☆ ☆ ☆

NOTES FOR NEXT TIME:

VISIT AGAIN?

YES   NO

PASSPORT STAMPS

KENAI FJORDS
NATIONAL PARK

CITY/STATE ENTERED:

DATES VISITED:

WEATHER:

WHO WAS WITH ME:

WHERE WE STAYED:

WHAT WE DID:

MY FAVORITE MEMORY

SIGHTS:

WILDLIFE:

HIKES/STORIES/ADVENTURES:

I WOULD RATE THIS NATIONAL PARK:

☆ ☆ ☆ ☆ ☆ ☆ ☆ ☆ ☆ ☆

NOTES FOR NEXT TIME:

VISIT AGAIN?

YES   NO

PASSPORT STAMPS

KINGS CANYON
NATIONAL PARK

CITY/STATE ENTERED:

DATES VISITED:

WEATHER:

WHO WAS WITH ME:

WHERE WE STAYED:

WHAT WE DID:

MY FAVORITE MEMORY

SIGHTS:

WILDLIFE:

HIKES/STORIES/ADVENTURES:

I WOULD RATE THIS NATIONAL PARK:

☆ ☆ ☆ ☆ ☆ ☆ ☆ ☆ ☆ ☆

NOTES FOR NEXT TIME:

VISIT
AGAIN?

YES   NO

PASSPORT STAMPS

KOBUK VALLEY
NATIONAL PARK

CITY/STATE ENTERED:

DATES VISITED:

WEATHER:

WHO WAS WITH ME:

WHERE WE STAYED:

WHAT WE DID:

MY FAVORITE MEMORY

SIGHTS:

WILDLIFE:

HIKES/STORIES/ADVENTURES:

I WOULD RATE THIS NATIONAL PARK:

☆ ☆ ☆ ☆ ☆ ☆ ☆ ☆ ☆ ☆

NOTES FOR NEXT TIME:

VISIT
AGAIN?

YES   NO

PASSPORT STAMPS

LAKE CLARK
NATIONAL PARK

CITY/STATE ENTERED:

DATES VISITED:

WEATHER:

WHO WAS WITH ME:

WHERE WE STAYED:

WHAT WE DID:

MY FAVORITE MEMORY

SIGHTS:

WILDLIFE:

HIKES/STORIES/ADVENTURES:

I WOULD RATE THIS NATIONAL PARK:

☆ ☆ ☆ ☆ ☆ ☆ ☆ ☆ ☆ ☆

NOTES FOR NEXT TIME:

VISIT
AGAIN?

YES   NO

PASSPORT STAMPS

LASSEN VOLCANIC
NATIONAL PARK

CITY/STATE ENTERED:

DATES VISITED:

WEATHER:

WHO WAS WITH ME:

WHERE WE STAYED:

WHAT WE DID:

MY FAVORITE MEMORY

SIGHTS:

WILDLIFE:

HIKES/STORIES/ADVENTURES:

I WOULD RATE THIS NATIONAL PARK:

☆ ☆ ☆ ☆ ☆ ☆ ☆ ☆ ☆ ☆

NOTES FOR NEXT TIME:

VISIT AGAIN?

YES   NO

PASSPORT STAMPS

MAMMOTH CAVE
NATIONAL PARK

CITY/STATE ENTERED:

DATES VISITED:

WEATHER:

WHO WAS WITH ME:

WHERE WE STAYED:

WHAT WE DID:

MY FAVORITE MEMORY

SIGHTS:

WILDLIFE:

HIKES/STORIES/ADVENTURES:

I WOULD RATE THIS NATIONAL PARK:

☆ ☆ ☆ ☆ ☆ ☆ ☆ ☆ ☆ ☆

NOTES FOR NEXT TIME:

VISIT AGAIN?

YES   NO

PASSPORT STAMPS

MESA VERDE
NATIONAL PARK

CITY/STATE ENTERED:

DATES VISITED:

WEATHER:

WHO WAS WITH ME:

WHERE WE STAYED:

WHAT WE DID:

MY FAVORITE MEMORY

SIGHTS:

WILDLIFE:

HIKES/STORIES/ADVENTURES:

I WOULD RATE THIS NATIONAL PARK:

☆ ☆ ☆ ☆ ☆ ☆ ☆ ☆ ☆ ☆

NOTES FOR NEXT TIME:

VISIT AGAIN?

YES   NO

PASSPORT STAMPS

MOUNT RAINIER
NATIONAL PARK

CITY/STATE ENTERED:

DATES VISITED:

WEATHER:

WHO WAS WITH ME:

WHERE WE STAYED:

WHAT WE DID:

MY FAVORITE MEMORY

SIGHTS:

WILDLIFE:

HIKES/STORIES/ADVENTURES:

I WOULD RATE THIS NATIONAL PARK:

☆ ☆ ☆ ☆ ☆ ☆ ☆ ☆ ☆ ☆

NOTES FOR NEXT TIME:

VISIT
AGAIN?

YES   NO

PASSPORT STAMPS

NORTH CASCADES
NATIONAL PARK

CITY/STATE ENTERED:

DATES VISITED:

WEATHER:

WHO WAS WITH ME:

WHERE WE STAYED:

WHAT WE DID:

MY FAVORITE MEMORY

SIGHTS:

WILDLIFE:

HIKES/STORIES/ADVENTURES:

I WOULD RATE THIS NATIONAL PARK:

☆ ☆ ☆ ☆ ☆ ☆ ☆ ☆ ☆ ☆

NOTES FOR NEXT TIME:

VISIT AGAIN?

YES   NO

PASSPORT STAMPS

OLYMPIC
NATIONAL PARK

CITY/STATE ENTERED:

DATES VISITED:

WEATHER:

WHO WAS WITH ME:

WHERE WE STAYED:

WHAT WE DID:

MY FAVORITE MEMORY

SIGHTS:

WILDLIFE:

HIKES/STORIES/ADVENTURES:

I WOULD RATE THIS NATIONAL PARK:

☆ ☆ ☆ ☆ ☆ ☆ ☆ ☆ ☆ ☆

NOTES FOR NEXT TIME:

VISIT AGAIN?

YES   NO

PASSPORT STAMPS

PETRIFIED FOREST
NATIONAL PARK

DATES VISITED:

WEATHER:

CITY/STATE ENTERED:

WHO WAS WITH ME:

WHERE WE STAYED:

WHAT WE DID:

MY FAVORITE MEMORY

SIGHTS:

WILDLIFE:

HIKES/STORIES/ADVENTURES:

I WOULD RATE THIS NATIONAL PARK:

☆ ☆ ☆ ☆ ☆ ☆ ☆ ☆ ☆ ☆

NOTES FOR NEXT TIME:

VISIT AGAIN?

YES   NO

PASSPORT STAMPS

PINNACLES
NATIONAL PARK

DATES VISITED:

CITY/STATE ENTERED:

WEATHER:

WHO WAS WITH ME:

WHERE WE STAYED:

WHAT WE DID:

MY FAVORITE MEMORY

SIGHTS:

WILDLIFE:

HIKES/STORIES/ADVENTURES:

I WOULD RATE THIS NATIONAL PARK:

☆ ☆ ☆ ☆ ☆ ☆ ☆ ☆ ☆ ☆

NOTES FOR NEXT TIME:

VISIT AGAIN?

YES   NO

PASSPORT STAMPS

REDWOOD
NATIONAL PARK

CITY/STATE ENTERED:

DATES VISITED:

WEATHER:

WHO WAS WITH ME:

WHERE WE STAYED:

WHAT WE DID:

MY FAVORITE MEMORY

SIGHTS:

WILDLIFE:

HIKES/STORIES/ADVENTURES:

I WOULD RATE THIS NATIONAL PARK:

☆ ☆ ☆ ☆ ☆ ☆ ☆ ☆ ☆ ☆

NOTES FOR NEXT TIME:

VISIT AGAIN?

YES   NO

PASSPORT STAMPS

ROCKY MOUNTAIN
NATIONAL PARK

DATES VISITED:

WEATHER:

CITY/STATE ENTERED:

WHO WAS WITH ME:

WHERE WE STAYED:

WHAT WE DID:

MY FAVORITE MEMORY

SIGHTS:

WILDLIFE:

HIKES/STORIES/ADVENTURES:

I WOULD RATE THIS NATIONAL PARK:

☆ ☆ ☆ ☆ ☆ ☆ ☆ ☆ ☆ ☆

NOTES FOR NEXT TIME:

VISIT AGAIN?

YES   NO

PASSPORT STAMPS

SAGUARO
NATIONAL PARK

CITY/STATE ENTERED:

DATES VISITED:

WEATHER:

WHO WAS WITH ME:

WHERE WE STAYED:

WHAT WE DID:

MY FAVORITE MEMORY

SIGHTS:

WILDLIFE:

HIKES/STORIES/ADVENTURES:

I WOULD RATE THIS NATIONAL PARK:

☆ ☆ ☆ ☆ ☆ ☆ ☆ ☆ ☆ ☆

NOTES FOR NEXT TIME:

VISIT AGAIN?

YES   NO

PASSPORT STAMPS

SEQUOIA
NATIONAL PARK

CITY/STATE ENTERED:

DATES VISITED:

WEATHER:

WHO WAS WITH ME:

WHERE WE STAYED:

WHAT WE DID:

MY FAVORITE MEMORY

SIGHTS:

WILDLIFE:

HIKES/STORIES/ADVENTURES:

I WOULD RATE THIS NATIONAL PARK:

☆ ☆ ☆ ☆ ☆ ☆ ☆ ☆ ☆ ☆

NOTES FOR NEXT TIME:

VISIT AGAIN?

YES   NO

PASSPORT STAMPS

SHENANDOAH
NATIONAL PARK

CITY/STATE ENTERED:

DATES VISITED:

WEATHER:

WHO WAS WITH ME:

WHERE WE STAYED:

WHAT WE DID:

MY FAVORITE MEMORY

SIGHTS:

WILDLIFE:

HIKES/STORIES/ADVENTURES:

I WOULD RATE THIS NATIONAL PARK:

☆ ☆ ☆ ☆ ☆ ☆ ☆ ☆ ☆ ☆

NOTES FOR NEXT TIME:

VISIT AGAIN?

YES   NO

PASSPORT STAMPS

THEODORE ROOSEVELT NATIONAL PARK

DATES VISITED:

CITY/STATE ENTERED:

WEATHER:

WHO WAS WITH ME:

WHERE WE STAYED:

WHAT WE DID:

MY FAVORITE MEMORY

SIGHTS:

WILDLIFE:

HIKES/STORIES/ADVENTURES:

I WOULD RATE THIS NATIONAL PARK:

☆ ☆ ☆ ☆ ☆ ☆ ☆ ☆ ☆ ☆

NOTES FOR NEXT TIME:

VISIT AGAIN?

YES   NO

PASSPORT STAMPS

VIRGIN ISLANDS
NATIONAL PARK

CITY/STATE ENTERED:

DATES VISITED:

WEATHER:

WHO WAS WITH ME:

WHERE WE STAYED:

WHAT WE DID:

MY FAVORITE MEMORY

SIGHTS:

WILDLIFE:

HIKES/STORIES/ADVENTURES:

I WOULD RATE THIS NATIONAL PARK:

☆ ☆ ☆ ☆ ☆ ☆ ☆ ☆ ☆ ☆

NOTES FOR NEXT TIME:

VISIT AGAIN?

YES   NO

PASSPORT STAMPS

VOYAGEURS
NATIONAL PARK

CITY/STATE ENTERED:

DATES VISITED:

WEATHER:

WHO WAS WITH ME:

WHERE WE STAYED:

WHAT WE DID:

MY FAVORITE MEMORY

SIGHTS:

WILDLIFE:

HIKES/STORIES/ADVENTURES:

I WOULD RATE THIS NATIONAL PARK:

☆ ☆ ☆ ☆ ☆ ☆ ☆ ☆ ☆ ☆

NOTES FOR NEXT TIME:

VISIT
AGAIN?

YES   NO

PASSPORT STAMPS

WIND CAVE
NATIONAL PARK

CITY/STATE ENTERED:

DATES VISITED:

WEATHER:

WHO WAS WITH ME:

WHERE WE STAYED:

WHAT WE DID:

MY FAVORITE MEMORY

SIGHTS:

WILDLIFE:

HIKES/STORIES/ADVENTURES:

I WOULD RATE THIS NATIONAL PARK:

☆ ☆ ☆ ☆ ☆ ☆ ☆ ☆ ☆ ☆

NOTES FOR NEXT TIME:

VISIT AGAIN?

YES   NO

PASSPORT STAMPS

WRANGELL-ST. ELIAS
NATIONAL PARK

CITY/STATE ENTERED:

DATES VISITED:

WEATHER:

WHO WAS WITH ME:

WHERE WE STAYED:

WHAT WE DID:

MY FAVORITE MEMORY

SIGHTS:

WILDLIFE:

HIKES/STORIES/ADVENTURES:

I WOULD RATE THIS NATIONAL PARK:

☆ ☆ ☆ ☆ ☆ ☆ ☆ ☆ ☆ ☆

NOTES FOR NEXT TIME:

VISIT AGAIN?

YES   NO

PASSPORT STAMPS

YELLOWSTONE
NATIONAL PARK

CITY/STATE ENTERED:

DATES VISITED:

WEATHER:

WHO WAS WITH ME:

WHERE WE STAYED:

WHAT WE DID:

MY FAVORITE MEMORY

SIGHTS:

WILDLIFE:

HIKES/STORIES/ADVENTURES:

I WOULD RATE THIS NATIONAL PARK:

☆ ☆ ☆ ☆ ☆ ☆ ☆ ☆ ☆ ☆

NOTES FOR NEXT TIME:

VISIT AGAIN?

YES   NO

PASSPORT STAMPS

YOSEMITE
NATIONAL PARK

CITY/STATE ENTERED:

DATES VISITED:

WEATHER:

WHO WAS WITH ME:

WHERE WE STAYED:

WHAT WE DID:

MY FAVORITE MEMORY

SIGHTS:

WILDLIFE:

HIKES/STORIES/ADVENTURES:

I WOULD RATE THIS NATIONAL PARK:

☆ ☆ ☆ ☆ ☆ ☆ ☆ ☆ ☆ ☆

NOTES FOR NEXT TIME:

VISIT AGAIN?

YES   NO

PASSPORT STAMPS

ZION
NATIONAL PARK

CITY/STATE ENTERED:

DATES VISITED:

WEATHER:

WHO WAS WITH ME:

WHERE WE STAYED:

WHAT WE DID:

MY FAVORITE MEMORY

SIGHTS:

WILDLIFE:

HIKES/STORIES/ADVENTURES:

I WOULD RATE THIS NATIONAL PARK:

☆ ☆ ☆ ☆ ☆ ☆ ☆ ☆ ☆ ☆

NOTES FOR NEXT TIME:

VISIT
AGAIN?

YES   NO

PASSPORT STAMPS

DATES VISITED:

CITY/STATE ENTERED:

WEATHER:

WHO WAS WITH ME:

WHERE WE STAYED:

WHAT WE DID:

MY FAVORITE MEMORY

SIGHTS:

WILDLIFE:

HIKES/STORIES/ADVENTURES:

I WOULD RATE THIS NATIONAL PARK:

☆ ☆ ☆ ☆ ☆ ☆ ☆ ☆ ☆ ☆

NOTES FOR NEXT TIME:

VISIT
AGAIN?

YES   NO

PASSPORT STAMPS

DATES VISITED:

CITY/STATE ENTERED:

WEATHER:

WHO WAS WITH ME:

WHERE WE STAYED:

WHAT WE DID:

MY FAVORITE MEMORY

SIGHTS:

WILDLIFE:

HIKES/STORIES/ADVENTURES:

I WOULD RATE THIS NATIONAL PARK:

☆ ☆ ☆ ☆ ☆ ☆ ☆ ☆ ☆ ☆

NOTES FOR NEXT TIME:

VISIT
AGAIN?

YES   NO

PASSPORT STAMPS

DATES VISITED:

CITY/STATE ENTERED:

WEATHER:

WHO WAS WITH ME:

WHERE WE STAYED:

WHAT WE DID:

MY FAVORITE MEMORY

SIGHTS:

WILDLIFE:

HIKES/STORIES/ADVENTURES:

I WOULD RATE THIS NATIONAL PARK:

☆ ☆ ☆ ☆ ☆ ☆ ☆ ☆ ☆ ☆

NOTES FOR NEXT TIME:

VISIT
AGAIN?

YES   NO

PASSPORT STAMPS

DATES VISITED:

CITY/STATE ENTERED:

WEATHER:

WHO WAS WITH ME:

WHERE WE STAYED:

WHAT WE DID:

MY FAVORITE MEMORY

SIGHTS:

WILDLIFE:

HIKES/STORIES/ADVENTURES:

I WOULD RATE THIS NATIONAL PARK:

☆ ☆ ☆ ☆ ☆ ☆ ☆ ☆ ☆ ☆

NOTES FOR NEXT TIME:

VISIT AGAIN?

YES   NO

PASSPORT STAMPS

DATES VISITED:

CITY/STATE ENTERED:

WEATHER:

WHO WAS WITH ME:

WHERE WE STAYED:

WHAT WE DID:

MY FAVORITE MEMORY

SIGHTS:

WILDLIFE:

HIKES/STORIES/ADVENTURES:

I WOULD RATE THIS NATIONAL PARK:

☆ ☆ ☆ ☆ ☆ ☆ ☆ ☆ ☆ ☆

NOTES FOR NEXT TIME:

VISIT
AGAIN?

YES   NO

PASSPORT STAMPS

Made in the USA
Coppell, TX
24 January 2020